A JANE AUSTEN

JOURNAL

With Notable Quotations from

Jane Austen

CHRONICLE BOOKS

SAN FRANCISCO

Her own
THOUGHTS

REFLECTIONS
were habitually
her best companions

Mansfield Park

*One's happiness
must in some measure
be always at the*

mercy

of

CHANCE

Sense and Sensibility

Her

manners were the

ЯОЯЯIM

of her own

modest

&

elegant mind

Henry Crawford, *Mansfield Park*

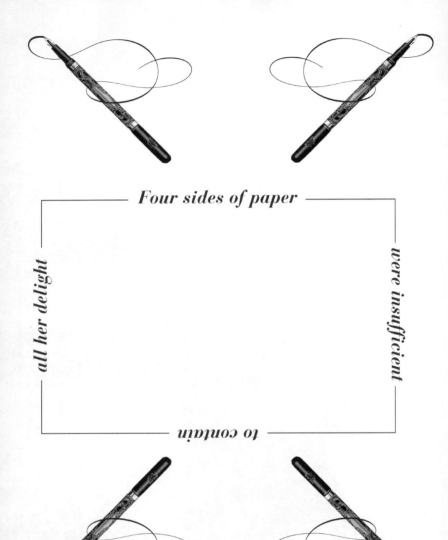

Four sides of paper — were insufficient — to contain — all her delight

Pride and Prejudice

If
I loved you

LESS

I might be able
to talk about it

Mr. Knightley, *Emma*

I

suppose

there may be a

HUNDRED

different ways

of being

in

Love Love

Emma Woodhouse, *Emma*

I
DID NOT
THEN KNOW

what it was to

Love

Willoughby, *Sense and Sensibility*

There could have been

no **2** *hearts* so open,

no tastes so similar,

no feelings

so in

UNISON

Persuasion

Not keep a

JOURNAL!

Henry Tilney, *Northanger Abbey*

ONE HALF OF THE WORLD

*cannot
understand
the pleasures
of the other*

Emma Woodhouse, *Emma*

Oh!

write, write.

Finish it at once.
Let there be an end of this suspense.

FIX  COMMIT ✹ CONDEMN

yourself.

Fanny Price, *Mansfield Park*

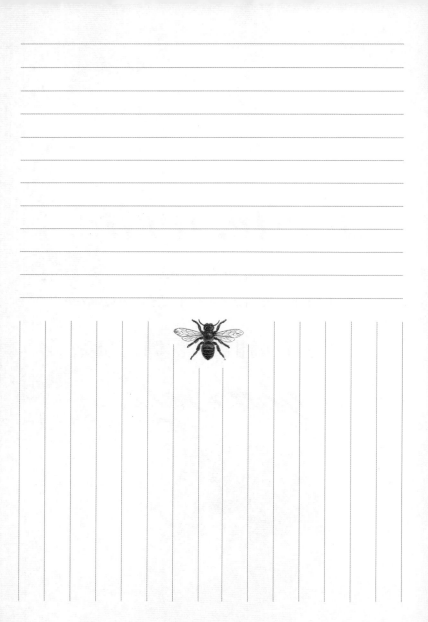

Wretched, wretched, mist ke!

Elizabeth Bennet, *Pride and Prejudice*

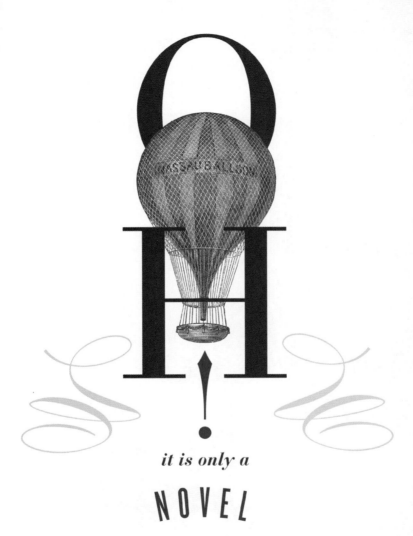

it is only a

NOVEL

Northanger Abbey

Let Other pens Dwell

on **guilt and misery**

Mansfield Park

There is no

Charm

equal to

tenderness of

Heart

Emma Woodhouse, *Emma*

These matters
are always a

secret

till it is found out that

EVERY BODY

knows them

Mr. Weston, *Emma*

To

FLATTER

*and follow others,
without being flattered
and followed in turn,
is but a state of*

$$\frac{1}{2}$$

enjoyment

Persuasion

MY

Feelings

**are at present
in a state of**

DREADFUL

InDECISION

Marianne Dashwood, *Sense and Sensibility*

Tell me not that I am *too late*

Captain Wentworth, *Persuasion*

Pray

WRITE TO HER

if it be only a

line

Henry Crawford, *Mansfield Park*

Till this
MOMENT

I NEVER KNEW
myself

Elizabeth Bennet, *Pride and Prejudice*

It is well
to have as many
HOLDS
upon
happiness
as possible

Henry Tilney, *Northanger Abbey*

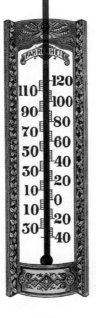

My

COURAGE

*always rises with
every attempt to
intimidate me*

Elizabeth Bennet, *Pride and Prejudice*

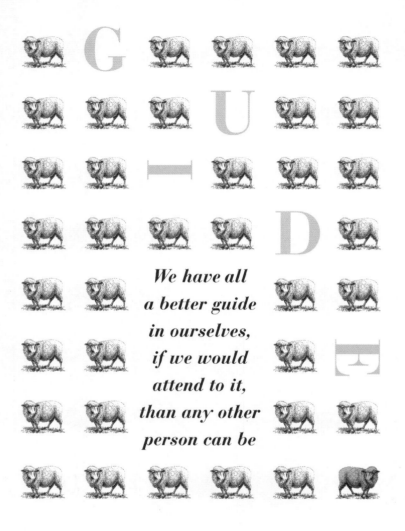

GUIDE

We have all
a better guide
in ourselves,
if we would
attend to it,
than any other
person can be

Fanny Price, *Mansfield Park*

I cannot be

FORCED

into genius

&

ELOQUENCE

Edward Ferrars, *Sense and Sensibility*

It is

A RULE WITH ME,

that a person who can write a long

Letter

with ease,

cannot

write

ill

Caroline Bingley, *Pride and Prejudice*

I think
there cannot be

TO

little said
on the

SUBJECT

Elizabeth Bennet, *Pride and Prejudice*

Her

happiness

was from

WITHIN

Persuasion

To understand,

thoroughly understand

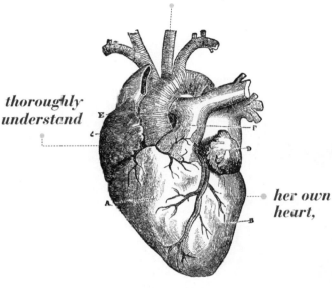

her own heart,

was the

FIRST

Emma

It is such a

HAPPINESS

when good people
get together

Miss Bates, *Emma*

I have Loved None but YOU

Captain Wentworth, *Persuasion*

**Think only
of the past
as its remembrance
gives you**

PLEASURE

Elizabeth Bennet, *Pride and Prejudice*

66 99

Jane's Papers Ltd. is a paper goods company founded by devout
Janeite Darby Walker, in collaboration with Los Angeles–
based creative directors Elaine Suh Bartlett and Brad Bartlett.
Together, they create stationery that brings together classic
literature, art, and typography.

ISBN 978-1-4521-1330-2

Manufactured in China.

Design by Elaine Suh Bartlett and Brad Bartlett.

10 9 8 7 6 5 4 3 2 1

Find more Jane Austen gifts
at www.chroniclebooks.com.

CHRONICLE BOOKS
680 SECOND STREET
SAN FRANCISCO, CA 94107
WWW.CHRONICLEBOOKS.COM